# SECRET DONUT

# SECRET DONUT

## AARON TIEGER

2009 : PRESSED WAFER : BOSTON, MASS.

# CONTENTS

*for Emily Belz*
*as promised*

# SUNDAY SHIFT

*after Bernadette Mayer*

November 6
65 degrees and we're thinking
of snow tires today
hail might hail
from the sunny sky


I like helping
            and I like
being helped

Feel slightly retarded
most days walking
to work
       w/pit
in guts
like going to school
       again
and again


       thinking
of the little kid
behind the hedge
in sun w/cat-
friend

O brother,
Sundays quaver
w/the palest blues
sung by man

cars and cats
and jobs and kids


        stars
     and blinking stars
     that look like planes


     dark park     half moon


       a heaven
   a gateway
a hope

"I want to go from
        operations
to corporate
one day"


    "I think
I'll be an art major"

The muse is not with me

What a stupid thing to say

I can't think
                    of anything
            but
auto
biography.

First snow before dawn
doesn't cover grass / mud
still it's snow quiet
chilly pretty morning

slow shift
garlands for the season
the bookstore's struggling


if it's Sunday it must be Bach
I have a new itch

Red head
red face
red handed

I lose my heart

it comes back
when she's gone

slow snow

slow day

slow head

wind

      picks up

day still drags

I have been neglectful
& now it's winter
                              snow
              garlands
holiday hours
still the store is slow

I control the music
                         and read

Magic 12
*Up to Speed*

$$\frac{\text{process}}{\text{product}}$$

new symbol for:
> *but what about*: progress
> $\neq$ project

Project

       project
much?

snow and sun and work
snow and sun
                and work
snow
        sun
work


muffin email smooth
jazz other desk work
er bitchy books
            water
            stare


                snow
        sun
& work

# TIME OFF

Summer bug
window bee
screen

I'm a high
wire bird
in dark

trees
times
skies

      between
here
there

snowflowers
cover roadside
fields

sun downs
lights
halo

smoketrees
lighter dark
trick cross

on a tight turn
certain bright
yellow fate

speed zone down

into town

All morning dreams
wrong upon waking
fade into rain

                     ocean

                            cities
& other dreams writing
down dreams kissed
by a poet TYPO
has a van & this
city is weird      St.
Louis w/red
light zone & coast
of roaring ocean

       big doings
many friends
chasing stills
from a film


Empty bed
embedded
memory
not so
strange
but for
the cats

Secret donut

    black sky

of a dozen stars

    black creek

frozen despite

        what lives be
            for
    me
          within
    me
        after

what remains
after the hook
gets pulled

sunshine and diamonds

    take a beautiful thing
    and call it black

In Aries now
spring shoots
up its shoots

open windows
of an evening
wind slowly
car quickly
                throughout
Collegetown Asian
girls litter
in the slow sun

Old guy dancing
to Errol Garner
in bookstore aisle


we're from the same
           place a road
connects in space
           & those towns
in time

a long time out
here w/no
word
from you there O
I've done it again

days of plans
days of work
days of sweat
       days
and days go on
       longer
than I've known

dreams of death
dreams of spies
dreams of friends
dreams of teeth
dreams of television
dreams of dragons
dreams of no dragons

face growing faster
hair getting longer
       cats

shedding up
      a storm

coming

any day

# NOISE

       people going
places doing
things turning
starting
machining
       & earning

Every space is
an ex space full
of important
productivity

inaudible per
mutations
of con
versations
constant bicker
between self
& something else

It's a jungle in there

It's a jungle in there
& things I care
about dwindle
in the mist
of things I do

Of myself
I ask
a lot
but
demand
not

Not just the bar
TV, not
the others, Pat
Benatar, not just
my contempt for them
but for me a part
of all this

A voice a tune a beat a
chord a strum a skronk
a sound
                    I
        recognize

each echo spells
a distant shore
            & speaks
a different truth

the space between

notes fills

space noise

needs

Physical, that
is in
the body
not head
noise but
vibe

        rationing

the quietness spreads
& stops

        like ink

Shaking
hands shaking
hell a deep
well running
low & a rock
rippling
long after
sunk

free time stands
all night &
all day
          taking
haymakers all
day & all
night
right
there
again I
had a good thought &
lost it

This ain't no
picnic or cage I
can't break
say A≠A or
always =
A

Rise above
like birds e.g.
*vs* and tildes
blurred on
smoky sky
            i.e.
mind

Lessons learned
again & over
head swells
w/lessons high
decibels of how
it goes

Relive the machine
decibel days &
decimal nights
machine reveals
& revives

Caffeine runs
machine dreams
Machinery dreams
w/programs run
automatic
as machines

What isn't is
not processed
process
by heart
or hand
tools trade fuel
for feeling real

Repetition is a form
of change

               repeating

change

               returning

change

               regressing

until changing

back

Under light
of city valley
rises chilly
to hill right out
of machinery
thick sky &
heart goes boom

# INN

*after Pierre Reverdy*

Closing eyes fast
dark wall thought
not emerging
Ideas
      leave
            step
by step

Dawn is over
before she starts
open blinds
fuck the morning

Shadow Ave. fading
seeing & retaining
      nothing

winds rise
stories close
days go out

If nothing should come
I know a field

# LOVE AGAIN

*after Pierre Reverdy*

A way toward vast
evening icy
shadows look
despair circles
toward formless
faces moving lines
imprison lines vague
eyes dim land
      scapes
      mystery
      days

Under cover weather
love by love burns
night / day
tired fixing
sighs turn
blue white
sands gold
wharf water
flatter
hard rock

Thought heavy sleep
blinking curls
nights without bed
too deep effects
tomorrow smile
sky slide hand
home    sick        solitude

O heart

                         sorrow

              never
used

# LYING DOWN

*after Robert Desnos*

Right left
sky sea
grass
flowers
right there

The clouds a road

Something happens
I don't care

Very vague
delirious
useless

# SAD LITTLE ROUND OF LIFE

*after Rene Daumal*

Heart rots
w / glimmer fear
evil heart
high & low

     Night
by holiday
night weak
heart broken
face

Beach breath
& windy tooth
Something drowns

Nobody
comes

# SPUTTERINGS

*after Blaise Cendrars*

Dissonant rainbows wire
less towers 12
to 12 everywhere
you hear it
*Shit.*


Chrome yellow sparks
Interweb nears
bells going off


Sing *No*
*Futurism*


They've stolen the stars
I wonder about the sky


Witches burning
on every corner

no horoscopes
you have to look

you have to work
I'm taking a trip


This one goes
out to you.

# WHITE HAUNCHES

*after Pierre Jean Jouve*

Happy underground
we're running around
lifting your dress
in bright red sun

singing azure
through drunk white teeth
with the birds
in silent times

## 2001, 2002, 2003

Excitement in the city
lights on side
walks through late
night exhaust cars
& noise

       living in a video
of growing up
stairs down
town sub
way stops
between tracks
singing w/beat
up beats in sub
terranean holes

everything a link
to a step to
a rung end
less climb
goes forever
is no end/

point

    inside

In the morning
      *people do this for years*
the subway slow
      hot
      or cold

everywhere we go
history
& nonhistory
conflate on the Ave.

3/22/06

Tiny snow
            again
        weather

has no bounds


I don't know what
anything
means
            but

people do have a way

# PIECES

*after Gil Scott-Heron*

I can see a 3
am 10
            years
past

            pieces
of a black soul/sky

where straight words
cut across        key
            pieces
of a letter
        a word
                    pieces
of a man

# COLORS AND THE KIDS

I wanted
        otherness
        to take me
from the colors
and the kids

A piano, repeating

What kept
me alive,
ever?

I still hear us crying
        buried
in this track
looping
        and
looping

          Matching
not the fact
but the voice
timbre          tone
& the same figure
two chords     repeating

When I was certain
I'd lost it       & needed
          someone
to become

Despair at bay &
heightened feelings
for kittens & kids

I don't want to die
or disappear
        dis-
assemble this
indefinite project

There is becoming

12/18/05


Geese honk
       & I love grey sky
Cold water runs through snow
in the creek
       & I love the sun

Something I never
       thought
I'd say
       &
must qualify
examine
test    but
still.

## READING TONY BAKER
### *SCRINS*

sleeping in the sun
on rug w/
       cat
& trees moving
       shadows
on window
       & me
not knowing
names of leaves
mushrooms grass
       etc.
       but
knowing

    what I have

& what I love

# ACKNOWLEDGMENTS

Most of "Sunday shift" first appeared in *Frame*. Thanks to Andrew Hughes. In addition "cars and cats" appeared in *Asterisk* and "snow and sun and work" appeared in *string of small machines*. Thanks to Jess Mynes and Luke Daly, Michael Slosek, Eric Unger, and Barrett Gordon.

"12/18/05" also appeared in *Asterisk*.

"Time off" appeared online in *Litter*. Thanks to Alan Baker.

Parts of "NOISE" appeared in *Effing* and online in *Skicka*. Thanks to Lars Palm.

"Colors and the kids" appeared in *small town*. Thanks to Logan Ryan Smith.